Pebble® Plus

Look Inside

Look Inside a Log Cabin

by Mari Schuh

Consulting Editor: Gail Saunders-Smith, PhD

Consultant: John Mark Lambertson
Director and Archivist
National Frontier Trails Museum
Independence, Missouri

Capstone

Mankato, Minnesota

Pebble Plus is published by Capstone Press,
151 Good Counsel Drive, P.O. Box 669, Mankato, Minnesota 56002.
www.capstonepress.com

1 2 3 4 5 6 14 13 12 11 10 09

Library of Congress Cataloging-in-Publication Data
Schuh, Mari C., 1975–
    Look inside a log cabin / by Mari Schuh.
    p. cm. — (Pebble plus. Look inside)
    Includes bibliographical references and index.
    Summary: "Simple text and photographs present American pioneer log cabins, their construction, and
their interaction with the environment" — Provided by publisher.
    ISBN-13: 978-1-4296-2246-2 (hardcover)
    ISBN-10: 1-4296-2246-6 (hardcover)
    1. Pioneers — Dwellings — United States — History — Juvenile literature. 2. Log cabins — United States
— History — Juvenile literature. 3. Log cabins — United States — Design and construction — History —
Juvenile literature. 4. Frontier and pioneer life — United States — Juvenile literature. I. Title.
E179.5.S34 2009
728.7'30973 — dc22   2008027654

Editorial Credits
Megan Peterson, editor; Renée T. Doyle, designer; Wanda Winch, photo researcher

Photo Credits
Alamy/Brad Mitchell, 13; Winston Fraser, 9
Capstone Press/Karon Dubke, 17, 21; Renée Doyle, back cover, 3
Gene K. Garrison Photography, 11
The Image Works/Jenny Hager, 15
North Wind Picture Archives, 7, 19
Shutterstock/Dmitry Kultayev, 24; Larisa Lofitskaya, 1, 22–23; Mary Terriberry, front cover; vectorgirl, flower
    design by page numbers
SuperStock, Inc./Richard Cummins, 5

Note to Parents and Teachers

The Look Inside set supports national social studies standards related to people, places, and culture. This book describes and illustrates log cabins. The images support early readers in understanding the text. The repetition of words and phrases helps early readers learn new words. This book also introduces early readers to subject-specific vocabulary words, which are defined in the Glossary section. Early readers may need assistance to read some words and to use the Table of Contents, Glossary, Read More, Internet Sites, and Index sections of the book.

Table of Contents

What Is a Log Cabin?

A log cabin is a small home made of tree trunks. American pioneers built them as they moved west starting in the mid-1700s.

Swedish pioneers built

the first log cabins

in America.

They showed other pioneers

how to build them.

Building a Log Cabin

To build a log cabin,

pioneers chopped down trees

with an ax.

Then they cut notches

in the ends of the logs.

Pioneers piled the logs to make walls. Then they used a process called chinking. They filled the wall spaces with mud, stones, and wood.

Pioneers built a roof
with flat pieces of wood.

Inside a Log Cabin

Most log cabins

had only one room.

Early cabins had windows

covered with oiled paper.

Later, windows were glass.

The floors were made
of dirt or wood.

Pioneers slept near the roof
in a loft.

A stone fireplace

kept the log cabin warm.

Pioneers cooked food

in the fireplace.

Log Cabins Today

You can learn about
log cabins at parks
and museums.
See how pioneers lived
in these strong wood homes.

Glossary

ax — a tool with a sharp blade on the end of a handle, used to chop wood

chinking — the process of filling spaces between rows of logs with mud, stones, and small pieces of wood

loft — a space with a floor under the roof of a building

notch — a cut shaped like the letter "U" or "V"; pioneers cut notches into the ends of logs so the logs would join together.

pioneer — a person who is among the first to settle in a new land

Swedish — people born in Sweden; Sweden is a country in northern Europe.

window — an opening in a building that lets in light

Read More

Rau, Dana Meachen. *Log Cabin.* The Inside Story. New York: Marshall Cavendish Benchmark, 2007.

Rea, Thelma. *Pioneer Families.* The Reading Room Collection. Social Studies. New York: PowerKids Press, 2006.

Internet Sites

FactHound offers a safe, fun way to find educator-approved Internet sites related to this book.

Here's what you do:

1. Visit *www.facthound.com*
2. Choose your grade level.
3. Begin your search.

This book's ID number is 9781429622462.

FactHound will fetch the best sites for you!

Index

Word Count: 163
Grade: 1
Early-Intervention Level: 17